THE B  F

Simon & Schuster
1230 Avenue of the Americas
New York, NY 10020

*The Best Life Diet* text copyright © 2006, 2009 by The Bestlife Corporation

*The Best Life Diet Cookbook* text copyright © 2009 by The Bestlife Corporation

Portions of this title were previously published in *The Best Life Diet* and *The Best Life Diet Cookbook*.

All rights reserved, including the right to reproduce this book or portions thereof in any form whatsoever. For information address Simon & Schuster Subsidiary Rights Department, 1230 Avenue of the Americas, New York, NY 10020

This Simon & Schuster edition October 2009

SIMON & SCHUSTER and colophon are registered trademarks of Simon & Schuster, Inc.

For information about special discounts for bulk purchases, please contact Simon & Schuster Special Sales at 1-866-506-1949 or business@simonandschuster.com.

The Simon & Schuster Speakers Bureau can bring authors to your live event. For more information or to book an event contact the Simon & Schuster Speakers Bureau at 1-866-248-3049 or visit our website at www.simonspeakers.com.

Manufactured in the United States of America

10 9 8 7 6 5 4 3 2 1

ISBN 978-1-4391-5265-2

# A FEW WORDS FROM OPRAH

▶ I feel like I've always known Bob Greene, though the truth is, it's only been fourteen years since we first met. My life has not been the same since that meeting; Bob changed my life.

At the time, I was 237 pounds, miserable, and so ashamed to have joined the ranks of the perpetually obese that I had trouble maintaining eye contact. I couldn't understand why I was able to triumph over so many other challenges and adversities in life, and yet when it came to losing weight I was a big fat failure.

Before I met Bob, I had spent years bouncing from one diet to another, beginning from the time I was twenty-two. That was the year that I landed a big job as a news coanchor in Baltimore and discovered that food—and especially corn dogs and six-inch chocolate-chip cookies with macadamia nuts from the mall food stalls—could provide a great deal of solace. I was naïve, felt very alone, and was having trouble adjusting to my new job.

I had no friends and no furniture, not even curtains on the windows of my new apartment. My coanchor seemed to resent me, and I worried that I was in way over my head. I'd had almost no experience as a writer, but every day I was given news copy to rewrite for my segment of the broadcast. In my previous job I had been more of a newsreader: the copy had been written for me and all I had to do was read it on air. It's an awful feeling when you know you can't make the mark. No matter how hard I tried, I could not bang out the copy fast enough for my superiors. Inevitably, every day as we neared the six o'clock news hour I'd hear John, the copy editor, yell across the room: "WINFREY, WHERE'S THE GODDAMNED COPY!!!!"

I was humiliated but put on a smile and got through the days, reading the news and chitchatting with my fellow anchors on air. But I didn't like my job. I felt blessed to have it, but I truly hated some of the things I was required to do. I always felt like I was chasing bodies, waiting for the worst to happen. The bigger the fire, the more bodies in the collision, the more devastating the natural disaster, the more excited my bosses became.

Working in that environment was an affront to my spirit; the reporter's objectivity I needed to maintain went against everything in my nature. Many times I was an eyewitness to the most devastating moments in people's lives, but I was not allowed to express any emotion. So I ate those emotions, and along with them just about everything I could buy at the food court. I thought I was just fine; I just had a little weight problem. Now I realize I didn't have a weight problem. I had problems that I was burying by eating, but it wasn't until years later, after many conversations with Bob, that I finally made the connection.

When all those corn dogs and chocolate-chip cookies finally pushed me up to 140 pounds—a weight I would do the hula in the streets for now—I went to my first diet doctor. I paid $27 for a consultation and an eating plan that called for 1,200 calories a day. It was my first time counting and cutting calories, so of course my young body responded well. I lost 7 pounds the first week, and in a month I was down to 125. Slim again, I started my old habit of grazing through the food stalls at the mall. My regular dinner plan: a baked potato with all the toppings—melted cheese, bacon, and chives—followed by one of those six-inch cookies from the Great American Cookies stand. In my freezer were stacks of Stouffer's macaroni and cheese, my comfort food of choice.

And so it went. I'd gain some, then I'd lose some. It was a cycle I'd end up repeating again and again.

When I first met Bob and he asked me why I was overweight, I thought he was being a smart-ass. I was overweight for the same reason everybody else is, I answered smugly. I loved food.

It took me a while to get to the truth. I didn't love food. I used food to numb my negative feelings. It didn't matter what the feeling was. A phone call from someone I didn't want to talk to; a confrontation of any kind; being late; feeling tired, anxious, or bored. No matter how insignificant the discomfort, my first reaction was to reach for something to eat: a grape, Cheerios, a handful of nuts, chips, popcorn. I'd eat, unaware of how much I was consuming, until I was chewing on the last kernels of corn. That's what it means to live unconsciously.

What I know for sure is that living an unconscious life is like being the walking dead. All my fat years—my unconscious years—are a blur to me now. It's only because I have photographs and diaries that I remember them at all. And sometimes even then I don't remember being present, because I wasn't really there.

I grew up believing that people with money didn't have problems. Or certainly none that money couldn't solve. Then, in 1986, my show went national. It changed the trajectory of my life. When I'd started my working life in Nashville and Baltimore, paying the rent and the electric bill and making payments on my car left me with just enough to buy groceries and get my hair done. Now I had more money than I'd ever imagined, and everybody wanted some. The first thing I did was to retire my mother and a cousin who helped take care of me when I was growing up. My father let me buy him a new house and a Mercedes, but he refused to quit working in his barbershop. He's still there.

Then everybody came out of the woodwork. Distant family members, who I barely knew, wanted me to completely take care of them or wanted to work for me. Relatives I hadn't seen since I was ten years old showed up demanding thousands of dollars "because we're family." Helping my family was something I wanted to do, but I didn't know how to handle the total strangers who came to Chicago claiming to have spent their last dime leaving a battering spouse, or the teenagers who'd run away from home.

The first year I helped almost everyone who asked me, family and strangers alike. It was stressful trying to figure out how much to give to whom, and before I knew it, they'd return for more. I was overwhelmed, but I never felt it. Once again, I just ate until I couldn't feel. By the end of the year I was 200 pounds.

In 1988, totally frustrated and up to 212 pounds, I turned to Optifast, a liquid diet supplement program. For four months, I ate not a single grape, nut, or other morsel of food. I lost fat—and muscle—and I dropped to 145 pounds.

Now I know that it's impossible to starve your body for four months, then feed it, and not expect to regain the weight. Your body doesn't want to starve, so it holds on to every ounce of fat in case you do another crazy thing like consuming only about 400 calories a day!

It would take seven more years of gaining, gaining, and countless attempts to follow diets that I wasn't really prepared to stick to before I discovered the truth. In the meantime, I was racing through two hundred shows a year. My entire life was work. I was leaving my apartment at six a.m. and getting home at ten at night. Eating. Sleeping. Repeating the cycle five days a week. My friends were my staff, and even when we weren't working, our lives still revolved around the show.

In 1992, I won another Emmy for Best Talk Show Host. I had prayed that Phil Donahue would win so that I wouldn't have to embarrass myself by rolling my fat butt out of my seat and walking down the aisle to the stage. By now I'd reached the end of believing I could be thin, though I was scheduled to leave for Colorado the next day to visit yet another spa. I was so depressed about my weight, I had little hope that I would be successful this time around. Every time the number on the scale went higher, it seemed even more hopeless. And 237 pounds was the heaviest I'd ever been. I had journals filled with prayers to God to help me conquer my weight demon.

Bob Greene was the answer to my prayers. When I first met Bob at that last-ditch-effort spa in Colorado, I thought for sure he was judging and labeling me as I had already judged and labeled myself: fat and out of control. Bob, it turned out, wasn't judging me at all. He really understood.

But he did have some tough questions for me. One of them was the hardest question that anyone has ever asked me: What is the best life possible for you? I remember one conversation in particular.

"You of all the people in the world can have your life be what you want; why don't you do it? What do you really want?" he asked.

"I want to be happy," I replied.

"'Happy' isn't a good-enough answer. What does that mean? Break it down for me. When was the last time you were really happy?"

"When I was filming *The Color Purple*, seven years ago."

"What about filming *The Color Purple* made you happy?"

I didn't have to think to answer. "Doing that work filled me up. I was playing a character that was meaningful to me, surrounded by the brilliance of Alice Walker, Quincy Jones, and Steven Spielberg. I was so charged and stimulated every day, I just wanted to do better and be better."

"So what would it take for you to have that feeling again?"

In answering that question, I realized the show had gotten away from me. In order to stay competitive, we had become more and more salacious, covering topics like "My sister slept with my husband" and "Is my husband or my boss my baby's father?" I didn't want to put junk on the air that perpetuated dysfunction instead of resolving it. It wasn't who I wanted to be.

And so, while I worked out and changed what and how much I ate, managing the rest of my life became my real focus. I started asking myself the same questions Bob had asked me. For every circumstance, I asked myself:

"What do I want?"

"What kind of show do I want?"

"What kind of body do I want?"

"What do I want to give to all the people who are asking me for my money, my attention, my time?"

I finally made a decision about that last one. I set up trust funds with a finite amount of cash for the people to whom I wanted to give money. And to those with whom I had no connection, I said no, and meant it. And just to be sure, I changed my home number. I've never visited a psychiatrist, but working with Bob has been priceless therapy.

Another thing I know for sure now is that you've got to ask yourself: What kind of life do *I* want and how close am I to living it? You cannot ever live the life of your dreams without coming face-to-face with the truth. Every unwanted pound creates another layer of lies. It's only when you peel back those layers that you will be set free: free to work out, free to eat responsibly, free to live the life you want and deserve to live. Tell the truth and you'll learn to eat to satisfy your physical hunger as opposed to your emotional hunger and to stop burying your hopes and dreams beneath layers of fat.

A young woman on my show who had been struggling with her weight once said to me she'd learned to challenge the pain and not the peanut butter. I thought that was brilliant. Once you work on what's eating you, you won't want to eat so much.

The Best Life Diet plan on the following pages mirrors the way I eat and live now. (You'll find a full week of my menus and some of my favorite foods here.) There is no secret to losing weight. It's simple physics: what you put in versus what you put out.

I lost weight in stages. First I became active: I still work out even though I really hate it, but I know if I don't, I will end up at 200 pounds again. Then I started working on my eating. First I stopped eating past 7:30 at night. When Bob told me it would make a big difference in my weight, I resisted. I thought it was going to be too hard. It was at first, but it gradually got easier. I rearranged my life so I wasn't rushing to make the 7:30 p.m. eating cutoff time. Not eating after 7:30 p.m. turned out to be one of the most effective changes I've made.

I've now taken most of the unhealthy foods out of my diet and replaced them with better choices. I eat smaller portions and healthful foods as a way of life, not as a diet to go on and off. I've even started a garden, and one of the most delightful moments for me these days is seeing a basket of just-picked green beans, tomatoes, lettuce, carrots, and corn sitting on my kitchen counter. And I'm always working on getting better. My diet is a work in progress.

Maybe what's most different now is that I think about *why* I eat, not just about what and how much. The truth is, most people—like me—have to keep watch on all three: why, what, and how we eat. We have to manage it daily. If you turn on the TV and see that I've picked up a few pounds, you will know that I'm not managing and balancing my life as well as I should.

I accept that mine is a very public life, although the

pain and frustration I experience when I gain weight is just as individual and difficult as your own. I still work constantly at not repressing my feelings with food.

One day I was leaving Santa Barbara, heading for Chicago. I was unable to fly due to bad weather, and I left the airport craving cake. I didn't process my feelings about being delayed; I just wanted cake. In particular, the coconut cake sold at the Montecito Café. Mind you, it was three years ago that I had my first and last bite of that cake, but the memory was so strong I could taste it. All the way home I thought about that cake.

I knew the café was closed, but I was still obsessing about it. I got home and stood in my pantry trying to come up with something that would substitute for the cake and satisfy my craving. I got out some pancake mix and a can of pineapple. I can make pineapple pancakes, add syrup, and it can taste kind of like the cake, I thought. I vowed to make a giant pancake right after I took my dogs for a walk.

While the dogs and I went for a long walk, I got really calm. I wasn't anxious about missing appointments and having to rearrange schedules anymore. I returned home and didn't even think about cake or pancakes, pineapple or syrup.

I started a new book, and went to sleep in peace.

Pausing is something I do more often now.

And I pray or meditate—or do both—every day. I

start my day with a prayer that Marianne Williamson shared in her book *Illuminata: A Return to Prayer.*

*Dear God,*
*I give this day to You.*
*May my mind stay centered on the things of spirit.*
*May I not be tempted to stray from love.*
*As I begin this day, I open to receive You.*
*Please enter where You already abide.*
*May my mind and heart be pure and true, and may I not deviate from the things of goodness.*
*May I see the love and innocence in all mankind, behind the masks we all wear and the illusions of this worldly plane.*
*I surrender to You my doings this day.*
*I ask only that they serve You and the healing of the world.*
*May I bring Your love and goodness with me, to give unto others wherever I go.*
*Make me the person You would have me be.*
*Direct my footsteps, and show me what You would have me do.*
*Make the world a safer, more beautiful place.*
*Bless all Your creatures.*
*Heal us all, and use me, dear Lord, that I might know the joy of being used by You.*
*Amen.*

I pray to be used by a power greater than myself. It takes consistent effort to live my best life.

The mistake I've made in the past is not realizing how constant a struggle it really is not to turn to food for comfort. It comes down to another question Bob asked me years ago: "How much do you love yourself?"

"Of course I love myself," I'd snapped. "It's the first law of self-preservation. I firmly believe in it."

"You may believe it, but you don't practice it," he said. "Otherwise you couldn't let yourself be two hundred and thirty-seven pounds."

I wanted to cry, and later I did. He was so right. I cared more about everyone else's feelings than my own. I'd overextend myself to do anything anyone asked, to honor his or her feelings. I didn't want anyone to think I wasn't "nice" or, worse, that "the money has gone to her head."

This, too, I know for sure: Loving yourself means honoring yourself and your own feelings *first*. When I was 237 pounds, I didn't even know what I felt. It was like living behind a veil of fat.

My hope is that you can learn from my mistakes and liberate yourself from this struggle. I finally know it doesn't have to be so hard. Make a decision. Know that you deserve the best life possible. It's there for the asking, the answering, the taking. Go out and get it!!!!!

*Opra*

# INTRODUCTION

▶ Losing weight is not that complicated. Eat fewer calories than you burn and the pounds will drop off, your clothes will loosen up, and you'll see a lower number on the scale. It's that simple. Only it never really is that simple. While the formula for weight loss may be uncomplicated, people are not. To varying degrees, we're all at the mercy of our physical yearnings, years of deeply ingrained habits, roller-coaster emotions, social pressures, and an inborn penchant for pleasure—in short, we all have our own human nature to contend with, and that has turned the relatively straightforward process of losing weight into a surprisingly complex problem.

I'm an exercise physiologist, so I've had a lot of training in how the human body operates. But my real education has come from being a student of diet successes and failures. *How* you lose weight is no great mystery—that's just a matter of eating fewer calories than you burn. The more puzzling question is *why*, after managing to shed at least some—or perhaps even a lot of—weight, so many people change course and return to their old ways.

After working one-on-one with many clients and talking to thousands of people through the years, I think I can say with some authority that the fast-and-furious approach to weight loss is also the fastest route to failure.

Here's why: human beings don't respond well to sudden changes. However, your body—and your mind—both have a powerful ability to adapt to change when it comes at you in measured amounts. Think about how athletes train. They don't immediately go from lifting 20 pounds to lifting 100 pounds, and they don't go from running 2 miles to running 26 miles overnight. Instead, they work up to the pinnacle of their capabilities, giving their bodies a chance to become accustomed to the new demands being placed on them. This step-by-step strategy makes sense when it comes to weight loss, too.

Change—or, I should say, lasting change—simply takes time. And that's not only true of how our bodies work, it's also true of how our minds work. If you've always relied on food for emotional sustenance, you will have to get used to the idea of turning to other things to help you through tough times. Perhaps most important, you've got to figure out *why* you need food to make yourself feel better. If you're eating because you're stressed, angry, bored, or lonely, you've got to find out what's at the root of those feelings and change it. That may take some time, but it's one of the most critical components of weight loss. For Oprah, becoming aware of and dealing with her habit of burying her emotions under plates of food was *the* most critical component. For many people, it will be as well.

# OFFERING YOU ONGOING SUPPORT

Whether it's grappling with emotional eating, improving your diet, or getting out and moving more, I can offer you lots of support. In addition to this booklet and game, there's the book, *The Best Life Diet*, and companion website, www.thebestlife.com. Both book and website are based on a three-phased approach to making the necessary changes that will drop pounds and keep them off. I'll be using the website to keep you abreast of everything from interesting new foods (including those bearing the Best Life seal and the Best Life Treat seal) to research news from the field of nutrition science. The Best Life team, which consists of an outstanding team of chefs, dietitians, doctors, exercise physiologists, and certified personal trainers, will be keeping an ear to the ground to give you frequent updates. And we'll also be out there scrutinizing store shelves, checking ingredients, and testing recipes. There will be articles about eating trends, an exercise library filled with great workouts, techniques for keeping you motivated, tools for self-discovery, and countless delicious recipes. This is a diet for life, so the last thing I want is for you to get tired of the foods you're eating or to miss out on news that can benefit your well-being. The world around us changes; the way you eat should change, too.

The website also has the ability to offer you individualized versions of the Best Life Diet with meal plans customized to the specifics you provide, whether you need ideas for vegetarian meals, an egg-free plan, or any one of a number of other dietary adjustments. The detailed feedback you get on your diet and exercise habits is almost like checking in with a dietitian or trainer. (In fact, you can write to our experts whenever you want and get a personalized answer.)

Another feature of www.thebestlife.com is that it can put you in touch with other people who are dealing with the same weight-loss challenges you are. Hooking you up with others in the program is another way the website can help you well beyond the pages of this book.

## LOOKING AT THE WHOLE PICTURE

It's not an accident that this program has the word *life* in its name. Losing weight can change your life for the better in ways that far exceed being happier with your appearance. It can even change your life in ways that you would not expect. So many people I've worked with have found that losing weight made them more open to trying new things and going to new places. They became more confident in social situations, too. And all of it—the new people, the new experiences, the new places—resulted in them eventually leading a life very different from the one they led before they shed the extra pounds.

The process you go through to lose weight can give you valuable insight into yourself and what it is that's preventing you from having the full life you want. What's more, each step you take toward reaching your weight-loss goal is really a gift that you give yourself. When you eat right and exercise, you are taking care of yourself, treating yourself with respect, and acknowledging that you deserve to be healthy and happy.

A crucial difference between this program and your typical "miracle" diet is that miracle diets tend to give you a big bang—maybe a quick or surprisingly substantial weight loss—that peters out fairly quickly. The beauty of this program is that it provides you with a series of ongoing victories. Each day you take a few small steps, then build on them the day after that. Sure, there may be setbacks—everyone has them—but those victories will add up, and pretty soon you'll be amazed at how different your life has become. And what could be more alluring than the prospect of waking up to your best life? So let's roll up our sleeves and get to work!

## INCREASE YOUR ACTIVITY

While it's possible to lose weight and keep it off without being active, it's very difficult—so difficult that not many people are ever really able to do it. One of the main benefits of activity is that it counters some of the negative effects of calorie reduction by helping to preserve muscle and prevent the body's natural inclination to slow your metabolism when faced with consuming less food. You'll learn more about both of these processes later in this section, but let's just say for now that there's a good reason why the people who are most successful at losing weight and maintaining weight loss do so through a combination of diet and exercise.

Experts in the weight-loss field have always maintained that pairing diet and exercise is the best approach to shedding pounds. If you haven't already incorporated activity into your life, I really urge you to do now. If you used to exercise and now you're on a sort of hiatus—maybe you had a baby and never returned to your regular workouts, or you got super busy at work and let your gym membership lapse—take this opportunity to get back on track. If you're already active, I hope you'll bump it up at least a level as part of your commitment to this program. The more you move your body, the easier losing weight on this—or any—weight-loss program is going to be.

Cutting calories can be challenging, so the fewer calories you have to eliminate from your diet, the better. This is where activity comes in. Exercise increases the number of calories you burn (in more ways than you may think), and that means you can eat more and still achieve the negative energy balance you need to lose weight. (Being able to eat more also increases the chances that you'll get all the nutrients you need.) When you're trying to cut back on the amount of food you eat, those extra calories can really feel like a windfall. And on this program, they really are a windfall because the more activity you incorporate into your day, the more Anything Goes Calories you'll get. These are treat calories to be "spent" on your favorite foods. If you move more, you can eat more, and if you can eat more, you'll be less stressed-out about feeling deprived.

If you break out of activity levels 0 and 1 and move up to Level 2 or higher (I'll tell you about activity levels later in this chapter) the rewards are particularly sweet. Research shows that there's a nice window of opportunity in the thirty minutes right after exercising to replenish your muscles with carbohydrates and protein. In this post-activity state, muscles act like sponges and absorb nutrients at a particularly high rate, so it's actually to your benefit to have a snack, such as a sweet yogurt shake, an energy or granola bar, some low-fat chocolate milk, a handful of chocolate-covered peanuts or almonds, some low-fat pudding, even a homemade milkshake made with one cup of fat-free milk and a heaping half cup of light ice cream.

Of course, this is not the only perk of exercise. Increasing your activity is going to make you feel more energetic, improve your mood, and boost your confidence in your own capabilities. Each of these things will contribute to your weight-loss efforts.

If you already exercise, you're getting some of these great benefits right now. However, the fact that you want to drop some weight despite being active means that you probably need to raise the bar a bit higher. If you fall on the opposite side of the spectrum and aren't very active (or aren't active at all), the rewards I just mentioned are in your future. All it's going to take is a very moderate increase each day in how much you move your body. It doesn't even have to be formal exercise; it can be that you just walk a couple thousand steps more each day. As long as you move more, you're going to benefit.

## THE WEIGHT-LOSS EDGE
## ONLY ACTIVITY CAN GIVE YOU

I'm sure you're very familiar with the fact that activity burns calories. Every time you move, whether you're taking a brisk forty-five-minute walk around your neighborhood, huffing away on an elliptical trainer for thirty minutes, strolling around the grocery store, or bending down to pick up laundry, you burn calories.

Activity actually has an "afterburn" effect—that is, it can raise your metabolism for hours after you've stopped exercising. Once you step off the treadmill, stop digging in your garden, or return home from a walk in the park, the rate at which you burn calories remains higher than usual and doesn't slow back down for quite some time. In this sense, you may think of activity kind of like money in a savings account. If you put a nice chunk of change in the bank then you earn interest on top of that without even lifting a finger. Likewise, you burn a good chunk of calories while exercising; then you get the bonus of burning more calories without any extra effort.

You get this post-exercise metabolism boost whenever you do any type of activity, whether it's aerobic exercise (which gets your heart rate up and accelerates your breathing), strength training with weights or bands, or other activities such as calisthenics, Pilates, or yoga. Some research has shown that one's metabolism can stay elevated for up to sixteen hours after exercise. Not surprisingly, the more vigorous your exercise, the longer the afterburn effect; however, even little bursts of activity, like walking up a few flights of stairs, can give your metabolism a small extended lift.

Activity also affects your metabolism by influencing the amount of muscle you have. Muscle is a very hungry tissue. It takes quite a few calories just for the body to maintain it, and the more muscle you have, the more calories you burn, even when you're just sitting around doing nothing. But muscle deteriorates naturally with age if you don't do anything to prevent it. Drastically cutting calories also puts muscle tissue at risk because when you eat less food, your body doesn't just turn to your fat stores for fuel but also feeds on your muscles.

Because muscle and metabolism are so intimately related, it's important that you keep the muscle tissue you have intact to prevent any slowdown in the rate at which you burn calories. It's even better if you can build additional muscle because that will raise your metabolism. Strength training is the best type of exercise for maintaining and adding muscle, but aerobic exercise helps your muscles burn calories at a higher rate. If you want to ensure that your body is burning calories at its maximum capacity, then including both aerobic exercise and strength training in your regimen is the ultimate way to go.

When you exercise, scores of physiological changes take place; activity literally alters the chemistry of your body. One of those changes is that your set point—the level of body fat that your body is programmed to maintain—drops. In other words, your body will carry less fat. Usually, if you significantly decrease the number of calories you eat, your metabolism will slow down. This is the body's defense mechanism to prevent starvation, passed down from our ancestors who lived in a time when rapid weight loss usually signaled something dire, such as famine. Times have changed, but the set point reflex hasn't.

When you exercise, the extra activity resets your "fat thermostat" so when you try to drop pounds, your body doesn't put up a big fight by slowing your metabolism. Instead, it allows you to lose more body fat than you would otherwise. You may eventually hit a weight-loss plateau; however, increasing your activity slightly once more can help you push past it again.

So let's recap: activity burns calories, allowing you to eat more food while still shedding pounds. It revs up your metabolism, increasing your energy expenditure above and beyond your normal capacity. It prevents the loss of muscle tissue, thereby counteracting an age- and/or calorie-cutting-related metabolic slowdown, and it lowers your fat thermostat. Could there possibly be a reason *not* to be active? I rest my case.

# ESTABLISHING YOUR ACTIVITY LEVEL

Everybody moves. What I want to help you do is move a little, preferably even a lot, more. First, though, you need to establish your starting point by locating your level of activity on the Best Life Activity Scale. I recommend that you read *all* of the levels and not stop reading once you find the category you fall into. That way you can get an idea of not only where you are on the continuum now, but also where you want to ultimately (and can realistically) go, both in the immediate future and further down the road.

## The Best Life Activity Scale

The Best Life Activity Scale is composed of six different levels of physical activity. You can gauge your activity level using either your weekly aerobic minutes or steps-per-day. Aerobic exercise is gauged by the number of minutes you spend exercising each day. (Remember that how hard you work out, or the intensity, is very important. You should be exercising vigorously enough that you're breathing deeply—you could still talk but would probably choose not to. And although you're feeling fatigued, you can still complete your regular workout. Maintaining this level throughout the entire workout will ensure that you're getting the full calorie-burning benefits of exercise. For more on gauging exercise intensity, check out www.thebestlife.com.) Steps per

▶ **More everyday energy.** People who exercise regularly simply have more energy. They move more and they move faster throughout the day, and as a result they burn a greater number of calories without even trying. If you're unfit, physical activity can make you feel more fatigued than usual. But after a few weeks, being active gives you renewed and enhanced vitality, and that translates into more everyday movement: getting up to grab something from your bedroom instead of asking one of your kids to bring it to you; pacing while you talk on the phone instead of sitting. Over the course of a day, all of those

day, as you would expect, measures the number of steps you take each day. To determine your steps—which includes all the steps you take while going about your daily activities and any steps you take while doing formal exercise, such as brisk walking or jogging—you'll need a pedometer, a clip-on counting device. You can purchase one at most sporting goods stores or on www .thebestlife.com.

Neither steps per day nor aerobic activity is interchangeable with strength training, which is part of lev-

little moves add up to a significant increase in energy expenditure. In the course of a year, that can add up to substantial weight loss.

▶ **Reduced appetite.** One other benefit of physical activity is that it often helps you tame your appetite. You may get a little hungrier if you exercise than if you don't (especially when you're just beginning an exercise regimen or are in the process of bumping it up a level), but not enough to compensate for the calories you'll burn through activity. You'll most likely still end up taking in less energy than you expend, causing weight to drop off.

els 3, 4, and 5, because they accomplish different goals. If you are at one of those levels, calculate how much strength training you do separately.

**Level 0** You're at Level 0 when any activity you do beyond what it takes to get through your day is purely accidental. Physical activity just isn't on your radar. You move only when you have to, and because of the way you've set up your life, that's not very often. You take the stairs only when the elevator is out of order, and anytime friends or family ask you to go for a walk, you find a convenient excuse to turn them down (wrong shoes, knee hurts, other commitments). You drive everywhere, maybe have a desk job, and usually just hang around on the couch at night, so your daily movement is minimal, which, you have to admit, is how you like it.

**AEROBIC EXERCISE:** none

*or*

**STEPS PER DAY:** 3,499 or less

**STRENGTH TRAINING:** none

**Level 1** You're at Level 1 if you see the value in activity, so you try to move as much as you can. You may have a job that keeps you on your feet—you're a nurse, waitress, landscaper, or teacher—or perhaps you just make an extra effort to move throughout the day. Maybe you often go for a stroll after dinner or ride bikes with your kids. At work, you'll walk to a colleague's office instead of using email, take the stairs when you can, and return your shopping cart to the front of the store instead of leaving it next to your car, just so you can get a few more steps in. Maybe you get off a stop or two early when you're taking public transportation and walk the rest of the way. You may be someone who hasn't participated in structured exercise since high school. Or maybe you used to have a regular workout program, but some change in your life such as having kids or sustaining an injury led you to quit, and you haven't picked it up again. In general, you look for creative ways to move more throughout the day.

**LIGHT AEROBIC EXERCISE:** up to 90 minutes per week

*or*

**STEPS PER DAY:** approximately 3,500–5,999

**STRENGTH TRAINING:** none

**Level 2** You're at Level 2 if you have a structured and consistent exercise schedule. It's fairly moderate, but it's helped you reap some cardiovascular, body-shaping, and calorie-burning benefits. You may work out any number of ways—by yourself on a stationary bike, in a kickboxing class at a gym, at home with an aerobics DVD, or with a fellow walker on the streets of your neighborhood—but you always get in at least three thirty-minute sessions a week.

**AEROBIC EXERCISE:** 3 times a week, 90–150 minutes per week

*or*

**STEPS PER DAY:** approximately 6,000–9,999

**STRENGTH TRAINING:** none

**Level 3** You're at Level 3 if you're serious about exercise and work out at least five and possibly six days a week. On at least four of those days, you do cardiovascular exercise—usually the same workout, whether it be walking, jogging, swimming, or something like going to a spinning or aerobic dance class—for a total of at least 150 minutes a week. At least two days a week, you strength-train with weights, performing at least six different exercises per session. You're so committed to activity that on the weekends, you also take leisurely but long walks.

> **AEROBIC EXERCISE:** 5 times a week, 150–250 minutes per week
>
> *or*
>
> **STEPS PER DAY:** approximately 10,000–13,999
>
> **STRENGTH TRAINING:** at least 2 times a week, a minimum of 6 exercises

**Level 4** You're at Level 4 if you not only work out almost every day, but also cross-train (engage in multiple aerobic activities) to get added benefits and to lower your risk for an overuse injury. For example, three days a week you run, walk, or use the elliptical trainer at the gym, and on another two days, you do aerobic activities like swimming, riding a bike, or taking an aerobics class. Altogether you rack up at least 250 minutes of aerobic exercise a week. You're also into strength training and do so consistently three days a week, performing at least eight different exercises per session. You may even use a challenging yoga or Pilates class to satisfy one of your strength-training workouts.

**AEROBIC EXERCISE:** 5 times a week, at least 250–360 minutes per week

*or*

**STEPS PER DAY:** approximately 14,000–17,999

**STRENGTH TRAINING:** at least 3 times a week, a minimum of 8 exercises

**Level 5** You're at Level 5 if exercise isn't just how you stay fit and healthy, it's a way of life. You may belong to a workout group, like a running, walking, or cycling club. Perhaps you challenge yourself by participating in races and competitions. You work out almost every day, maybe doing your main workout three times a week and cross-training three other days for a total of six hours of cardiovascular exercise a week. You've been strength training for some time now, and you're up to at least ten different exercises, a minimum of three days a week.

**AEROBIC EXERCISE:** 6 times a week, 360 minutes or more per week (Note: 360 minutes is a minimum; many people at this level are working out significantly more, even double this amount.)

*or*

**STEPS PER DAY:** approximately 18,000 or above

**STRENGTH TRAINING:** at least 3 times a week, a minimum of 10 exercises

## GOING TO THE NEXT LEVEL

Bumping up your activity level is a good idea no matter where you fall on the activity scale, but if you're at Level 0, it's critical. Your inactivity is a detriment to your health, and all the weight loss in the world isn't going to change that.

Going from Activity Level 0 to Level 1 isn't difficult. Level 1 really doesn't even make any substantial demands on your schedule. Actually, it would be far better if you skipped Level 1 and just went straight to Level 2, which will give you far greater benefits than Level 1 and allow you to increase your calorie intake, too. Just be sure that if you've never engaged in formal workouts, or haven't done so in some time, you check with your physician before you jump to Level 2. If you were once an exerciser and stopped, you'll be surprised how easy it is to get back into it.

If you are already exercising regularly and fall into Level 2 or above, your best bet is to move up one level at a time: increasing your exercise in increments will give your body time to adapt to the changes. But, if you're at Level 0, it's okay to start engaging in formal workouts

(Level 2 or higher), after checking with your physician, and I encourage you to do that.

It's *very* important that you select a level of activity that you can see yourself doing for the rest of your life. I don't want you to set your sights on a goal only to realize that it's impossible given your other commitments and responsibilities. (Check out the Food and Exercise Planner on www.thebestlife.com; it's a great tool that can help you find the time to work out even during your most hectic weeks.) If you're not willing to prioritize exercise right now, be honest with yourself. Choose to do as much as you're capable of doing instead of setting goals you can't meet.

It's not that I don't want you to aim high; on the contrary, I hope you will become an avid exerciser and perhaps even go all the way up to Level 5. But if you're unable to meet the activity goals that you set, you may end up doing no exercise at all, and that's the last thing you (or I) want to happen. You can even break up your workouts: do your cardio in the morning and strength training later on if it makes it easier to get it all done. But if none of these scheduling ideas is going to make a difference for you, I'd rather have you set your sights lower and do *something*—even if it's a ten-minute walk around the neighborhood—rather than be overly ambitious and end up doing nothing at all. Get it right in the beginning so that you end up with an activity regimen that will last a lifetime.

# CREATING CHANGE

*If you think you can or you think you can't, you're right.*
— HENRY FORD

▶ I've been helping people make lifestyle changes for over twenty-five years, and one thing is very clear: changing our behavior is one of the toughest things we can do. Changing how we eat is particularly tough due to our primitive hardwiring. We're born with mechanisms that make us want to eat high-calorie foods—and lots of them!

With the right approach, we can overcome those instincts. The tougher challenge is another kind of hardwiring: negative, firmly ingrained attitudes about the world and ourselves that were formed when we were growing up. If you're hampered by a negative attitude, you're going to need to think differently. Change your attitude and you can change your life, too.

By making exercise fun, this game can help change any negative feelings you might have about physical activity. In the complete *Best Life Diet* program, found in my book and website, I'm hoping to change more than just your attitude toward exercise. I also ask you to change when you eat, what you eat, and what you drink. I also ask you to set about changing the areas of your life that are troubled or in which you are unfulfilled so you will stop turning to food for comfort. You are capable of all of these things, but only if you believe you are. If there's one thing that people who make major—and permanent—changes in their lives have in common, it's a positive outlook.

Here's what it takes to be the optimistic and confident person you need to be to succeed: Focus on the good things that happen in your life each day rather than the bad. What went right today? What things did you do to benefit yourself? This doesn't mean that you need to avoid thinking about what went wrong; going over what you would have done differently is the best way to learn. But look at those things as something you can work to change, and vow to do better tomorrow.

Having a positive attitude prepares you to take the next steps toward change. Those steps are:

- ▸ Decide what you really want for your life.

- ▸ Make an honest assessment of yourself and what you're willing to change about yourself and your behavior.

- ▸ Determine what you need to do to accomplish those changes.

▶ Muster up the discipline needed to make it all happen.

▶ Avoid getting discouraged along the way.

▶ Find fulfillment out of each small step you take toward your Best Life.

Look at obstacles as opportunities and at challenges as a chance to show your mettle. In other words, take pleasure in persevering; that's what separates those people who keep pushing forward from those who throw in the towel. From what I've observed, people who persevere delight in each small victory. To them, having the inner strength to turn down a piece of cake at a party is cause for celebration. They feel good about themselves for their self-discipline—and their self-esteem, along with their motivation, grows. Perseverance is born out of affirming each small accomplishment along the way to a larger goal. That's what is going to help you develop the optimism you need to succeed.

If there is any secret to success, it's this: Be honest with yourself and those around you. Take responsibility for your actions and your life. Think of the commitments you make to yourself as sacred, and honor them in the way that you honor your commitments to other people. Identify what it is you really want from life, realize you deserve it, and think positively about your ability to get it. Make your plan, have the inner strength to stick to it, and claim the life you deserve!

# A MEAL-PLANNING PRIMER

▶ Eating is meant to be one of life's great pleasures. The simple act of sitting down to a meal can bring us joy, satisfaction, and, of course, nourishment; in a word, fulfillment—both physical *and* emotional.

Unfortunately, so many of us have lost that special connection with the experience of eating. Our busy schedules have prevented us from savoring the act of sitting down to a meal, whether it's just yourself or with those you care about. *The Best Life Diet Cookbook* can help: you can reclaim the experience of eating as a celebration by sitting down to enjoy the book's high-quality, delicious dishes without overdoing it. I've included seven days of meal plans at the 1700-calorie-a-day level from my cookbook, as well as a few recipes. You can follow the plan as is, or mix and match; for instance, you can choose any breakfast from any of the seven days, and pair it with any lunch, dinner, snack, or treat. (For many more recipes and weeks of meal plans, open up either of my books or log on to thebestlife.com.)

I hope that you'll come to think of eating healthy, home-cooked meals as a gift that you give to yourself and your loved ones. I encourage you to try to think of whipping up a nutritious meal not as just another task you have to do at the end of a busy day, but as a ritual that provides important vitamins and minerals, promotes good health, and gives you a wonderful opportunity to spend quality time with your family. Nourishing yourself and your loved ones, with great, healthy foods, is simply one of the most effective ways to satisfy the body and soul.

I know that many people just don't have a lot of extra time to cook a meal, and I took that into consideration when choosing the dishes to include in *The Best Life Diet Cookbook*. But the majority of the recipes here take just 30 minutes or less, and they include ingredients that you likely already have in your kitchen or can easily find at your local grocery store.

The cookbook will help you get back on track in the kitchen, and still leave you with plenty of time to get through everything on your to-do list. But I know that time isn't your only concern when it comes to eating; many of us have also become very calorie-conscious. For those of you who are trying to maintain your weight or slim down, these recipes will also help you focus on the quality of your food instead of the quantity. When you use fresh, high-quality foods, you won't have to eat as much to get that taste payoff. You'll be satisfied with less food, which means you'll consume fewer calories each time you sit down to eat.

The seven sample days included in this booklet come from the "Quick and Easy" meal plan in *The Best*

*Life Diet Cookbook.* (There's also a "Kitchen Connoisseur" and a "Family Friendly" plan.) No matter which plan you choose, you can be confident that you'll be getting all the nutrients you need. Each meal has been composed to ensure that you get the perfect balance of fat, carbs, and protein, and the plans are rich in vitamins, minerals, and phytonutrients. Why is this so important? Often, when someone fills up on empty calories (like a mound of French fries) or even has a relatively healthy dish that's missing a satisfying element, such as a whole grain roll, brown rice, or other complex carbohydrate, they tend to be more prone to grazing or snacking throughout the day. The end result: they take in more calories. These meals, on the other hand, will keep you satisfied and full, and will therefore help you cut your calorie intake.

With each recipe, you'll be reminded that eating is about so much more than simply satisfying your hunger. Cooking and enjoying healthy meals is a great way to take care of yourself and your family. I'm hoping you'll find a little more joy in cooking, a little more satisfaction in eating, a little more nutrition in your meals, and a little more time to sit down and experience the smells, flavors, and textures of your food. I want you to discover the pleasure of eating again and to allow healthy foods to enrich your life. The recipes in this booklet can play a part in helping you achieve this wonderful and fulfilling experience.

# QUICK AND EASY MEAL PLAN

▶ On this plan, you get the benefits of home-cooked meals without having to spend hours in the kitchen. You'll see a combination of quick from-scratch dishes paired with convenience foods (case in point: Day 1 dinner has both canned soup and Rotisserie Chicken Salad with Oranges and Pistachios). There are even some fast-food meals thrown in the mix. It's a plan that fits into—and fuels—your busy lifestyle.

**LS** = low sodium
**V** = vegetarian

## WEEK 1

### MONDAY, DAY 1

**BREAKFAST** LS V

▶ 190 calories of whole grain cereal (with at least 3 g fiber per 100 calories), such as 1 cup Cascadian Farm

Great Measure Cereal, topped with 2 tablespoons unsalted walnuts, pecans, or other nuts of your choice, and 1 cup fat-free milk

▸ ¾ cup strawberries or other berries

## LUNCH v

▸ Cheese and tomato sandwich: Spread 2 slices whole wheat bread with 1 tablespoon Hellmann's Canola Cholesterol Free Mayonnaise. Fill with 2 ounces (2 slices) reduced-fat Cheddar, such as Cabot 50% or reduced-fat Swiss or Jack, and 2 tomato slices. Add chopped fresh basil or other herb, if desired.

▸ Have the rest of the tomato (use 1 medium or large tomato) sliced, sprinkled with a dash of salt, and a drizzle of balsamic vinegar

▸ 1 apple

## DINNER

▸ 1 cup lentil or black bean soup (with 500 mg sodium per cup or less)

▸ 90 calories of any whole grain cracker

▸ 1 serving Rotisserie Chicken Salad with Oranges and Pistachios (page 51)

## HIGH-CALCIUM SNACK LS V

▸ 12-ounce fat-free milk latte, or 8-ounce glass of fat-free milk. Add 2 tablespoons unsalted nuts of your choice.

## TREAT (*anytime during the day*) LS V

▸ 150 calories of a sweetened nut mixture or bar, such as ¼ cup True North Peanut Crunches Honey Wheat

### TUESDAY, DAY 2

## BREAKFAST LS V

▸ Peanut Butter Banana Smoothie (page 52)

## LUNCH V

▸ 90 calories of any whole grain cracker, such as 2 pieces Wasa Multi Grain crispbreads, topped with ½ cup nonfat ricotta, 5 chopped olives, and 6 slices tomato, drizzled with 2 teaspoons olive oil

▸ 2 cups mixed greens and 1 chopped red pepper tossed with 10 sprays Wish-Bone Salad Spritzer, any flavor, and topped with 1 tablespoon toasted pine nuts or other nuts of your choice

## DINNER LS

▸ Broil a 5-ounce piece of fish (trout, salmon, mackerel, or other fish of your choice).

▸ 1 serving Raw Garlicky Kale (page 53)

▸ Garlic bread: 2 slices whole wheat bread with 2 teaspoons healthy spread, a smear of crushed garlic or a sprinkle of garlic salt, and a dash of black pepper. Heat in a toaster oven or oven until golden.

▸ ½ cup berries

## HIGH-CALCIUM SNACK LS V

▸ 1 Slim-Fast Optima Shake, any flavor

## TREAT (*anytime during the day*) LS V

▸ 150 calories of vegetable chips, such as Terra Sweet Potato or Sweets and Beets Chips (1 ounce, about 17 chips)

### WEDNESDAY, DAY 3

## BREAKFAST LS V

▸ Crunchy Yogurt with Fruit and Nuts (page 54)

## LUNCH

**NOTE:** This, like other fast-food meals, is high in sodium, so have it only occasionally.

▶ Fast-food lunch: Wendy's Small Chili, Side Salad with 1 packet Reduced-Fat Creamy Ranch Dressing, and a side of Mandarin oranges

## DINNER LS

▶ 1 serving Buffalo with Blackberries (page 55)

▶ 1 cup raw sweet potato sticks spritzed with olive or canola oil cooking spray, seasoned with a dash of salt and any herbs of your choice, and baked at 400°F for 25 to 30 minutes. Or use frozen sweet potato sticks, such as Alexia brand.

▶ 2 cups mixed greens, 1 cup chopped vegetable of your choice tossed with 1 tablespoon olive oil and 1 teaspoon balsamic vinegar. Top with 1 tablespoon walnuts.

## HIGH-CALCIUM SNACK V

▶ 60 calories' worth of whole grain crackers, such as 2 slices Wasa Fiber Rye Crispbread, spread with ½ cup nonfat ricotta cheese and topped with 6 olives

## TREAT (*anytime during the day*) LS V

▶ 3 tablespoons chocolate-covered peanuts

**BREAKFAST** LS V

▸ Oatmeal, ½ cup dry regular or ¼ cup steel-cut (Quaker, Arrowhead Mills, and McCann's make quick-cooking steel-cut). Top with 1 small apple, chopped; 1 tablespoon unsalted nuts of your choice; and 2 teaspoons brown sugar.

▸ 1 cup fat-free milk

**LUNCH** LS

▸ Chicken wrap. In a 90- or 100-calorie whole grain wrap or tortilla, such as Flatout Flatbread, place the following mix: ½ cup precooked chicken strips (or pieces pulled from a rotisserie chicken) mixed with 1 tablespoon Hellmann's Canola Cholesterol Free Mayonnaise, 2 teaspoons mustard, and 3 tablespoons finely chopped shredded carrots (or mushrooms or celery or a combo of all; whatever you can find prechopped at the grocery store or have time to chop yourself)

▸ 1 cup grapes and 1 tablespoon unsalted nuts of your choice

**DINNER**

▸ Lean Cuisine Spa Cuisine Gourmet Mushroom Pizza, 1 package

- 1 serving Roasted Broccoli with Balsamic Vinegar (page 57)

- 1 cup fresh blueberries, or frozen, thawed, with 2 tablespoons slivered almonds

## HIGH-CALCIUM SNACK LS V

- Celery with Creamy Herb Dip (page 58)

## TREAT *(anytime during the day)* LS V

- One 100- to 110-calorie biscotti, such as Nonni's, with 1 café au lait: ½ cup hot fat-free milk mixed with ½ cup hot coffee (decaf or regular)

### FRIDAY, DAY 5

## BREAKFAST LS V

- 1 slice whole wheat bread spread with 1 tablespoon nut butter, such as Smart Balance Peanut Butter, and topped with ½ banana, sliced. Drizzle with 1 teaspoon honey.

- 1 cup strawberries and ½ cup blueberries or other berries

- 1 cup fat-free milk (plain, or as part of a latte or heated and mixed with regular coffee)

## LUNCH v

▸ 1 cup minestrone soup (with no more than 500 mg sodium per cup), simmered with 1½ cups spinach

▸ 90 calories of any whole grain crackers, such as 2 pieces Wasa Multi Grain crispbreads, topped with 6 tablespoons nonfat ricotta, 1 tablespoon olive oil, and sprinkled with chopped fresh basil, parsley, or dill

▸ ½ cup sliced strawberries

## DINNER LS

▸ ¼ cup dry whole wheat couscous (use regular if you can't find whole wheat), cooked according to package directions, mixed with 1 teaspoon olive oil and topped with ½ tablespoon toasted pine nuts or slivered almonds

▸ 1 serving Poached Wild Salmon with Zucchini and Mustard (page 59)

## HIGH-CALCIUM SNACK LS V

▸ ¾ cup nonfat plain yogurt mixed with 3 tablespoons dried fruit

## TREAT (*anytime during the day*) LS V

▸ 2 Edy's or Dreyer's fruit bars (160 calories)

## BREAKFAST V

- ½ cup liquid eggs, such as Better'n Eggs, scrambled in 2 teaspoons healthy spread, rolled in 1 whole wheat wrap or tortilla, such as Flatout Flatbread Multi-Grain, with 2 tablespoons salsa

- 1 cup fat-free milk

- 1 grapefruit

## LUNCH

- Frozen meal (with around 400 calories, at least 3 grams of fiber, and no more than 4 grams of saturated fat), such as Lean Cuisine Chicken Fettuccine

- 2 cups mixed greens topped with 10 sprays Wish-Bone Salad Spritzers

## DINNER LS V

- 1 serving Angel Hair Pasta with Walnuts and Peas (page 61)

- Salad: 2 cups mixed greens tossed with 100 calories of regular dressing

## HIGH-CALCIUM SNACK LS V

▸ 1 cup Silk Vanilla Soymilk or fat-free milk and 1 cup peach slices

## TREAT  (*anytime during the day*) LS V

▸ Banana cream pudding: Slice ½ banana and layer with 1 fat-free vanilla pudding cup

### SUNDAY, DAY 7

## BREAKFAST LS V

▸ 2 whole grain toaster waffles (about 170 calories for the 2, such as Kashi), topped with 1 teaspoon healthy spread, 1 cup berries, and 1 tablespoon maple syrup

▸ 1 cup fat-free milk

## LUNCH V

▸ 1 cup reduced-sodium canned tomato soup

▸ 1 whole wheat pita stuffed with ½ cup chickpeas, 1 tablespoon chopped parsley, and 100 calories of vinaigrette dressing

## DINNER LS

▸ 1 serving Pan-Roasted Shrimp with Lemon, Garlic, and Spinach (page 62)

▸ Salad: 3 cups mixed greens, 1 cup chopped vegetables, such as tomatoes or red peppers, and 1 tablespoon toasted pine nuts or other nuts of your choice tossed with 1 tablespoon olive oil and 1 teaspoon balsamic vinegar

▸ 1 slice whole grain bread or roll (around 75 calories) with 2 teaspoons healthy spread

## HIGH-CALCIUM SNACK LS V

▸ 1 Luna Bar (with 180 calories, 35% DV for calcium)

## TREAT *(anytime during the day)* LS V

▸ 150 calories of light ice cream, about ¾ cup

# Rotisserie Chicken Salad with Oranges and Pistachios

*Serves 4*

TIRED OF HAVING rotisserie chicken with the standard sides? Try this fuss-free recipe, which is both flavorful and unique.

2 ½ pounds rotisserie chicken, skin removed, meat peeled from bone and roughly chopped (yields 3 to 3 ½ cups chopped chicken meat)

2 oranges, peeled and sectioned

1 tablespoon finely chopped red onion

1 tablespoon olive oil

1 tablespoon sherry vinegar

⅛ teaspoon salt

Black pepper to taste

4 cups romaine, chopped

¼ cup pistachios, toasted and roughly chopped

1. Combine the chicken, oranges, red onion, oil, vinegar, salt, and pepper in a large bowl. Set aside for 5 to 10 minutes.
2. Add the greens and pistachios and toss gently.
3. Divide among 4 plates and serve.

PREP TIME: 15 minutes    TOTAL TIME: 15 minutes

PER SERVING, ABOUT: Calories: 315  Protein: 36 g
Carbohydrate: 12 g  Dietary Fiber: 3 g  Sugars: 7 g
Total Fat: 14 g  Saturated Fat: 3 g  Cholesterol: 101 mg
Calcium: 67 mg  Sodium: 433 mg

# Peanut Butter Banana Smoothie

*Serves 1*

WHIPPING UP THIS quick recipe is a deliciously satisfying way to start your day. In fact, it's an entire meal in a shake!

1 frozen banana

2 tablespoons ground flaxseeds

1 tablespoon chunky peanut butter, such as Smart Balance

1 cup light vanilla soymilk, such as Silk

¼ cup liquid egg whites, such as AllWhites

Combine all the ingredients in a blender until smooth, about 2 minutes. Serve.

PREP TIME: 5 minutes   TOTAL TIME: 5 minutes

PER SERVING, ABOUT: Calories: 416  Protein: 21 g
Carbohydrate: 46 g  Dietary Fiber: 9 g  Sugars: 22 g
Total Fat: 18 g  Saturated Fat: 2 g  Cholesterol: 1 mg
Calcium: 371 mg  Sodium: 268 mg

# Raw Garlicky Kale

*Serves 4*

THIS IS A great way to eat your greens! These simple ingredients combine to make a remarkable dish. It's such a favorite that you'll find it more than once in the meal plans.

2 tablespoons tahini

4 cloves roasted garlic

2 tablespoons cider vinegar

1 tablespoon water

⅛ teaspoon salt

Fresh hot red pepper to taste

4 cups raw kale, cut into extremely thin strips lengthwise, well washed

1. Combine the tahini, garlic, vinegar, water, salt, and hot pepper in a food processor and puree until smooth, about 1 minute.
2. Toss the kale and tahini dressing together. Serve immediately or refrigerate for several hours before serving.

PREP TIME: 10 minutes    TOTAL TIME: 10 minutes

PER SERVING, ABOUT: Calories: 87 Protein: 4 g
Carbohydrate: 10 g Dietary Fiber: 2 g Sugars: 0 g
Total Fat: 5 g Saturated Fat: 1 g Cholesterol: 0 mg
Calcium: 173 mg Sodium: 103 mg

# Crunchy Yogurt with Fruit and Nuts
*Serves 1*

THIS RECIPE MAKES a well-balanced, one-dish breakfast. It covers nearly 50 percent of your calcium needs (for those age 50 and under), and the walnuts give you a nice dose of omega-3 fats.

6 ounces light yogurt (blueberry, Key lime, or apple)

½ cup plain nonfat yogurt

1⅓ cups fresh fruit sliced (berries and banana for blueberry yogurt; mango, orange, and banana for Key lime yogurt; apple, pear, and banana for apple yogurt)

1 crispbread, such as Wasa Light Rye, Multi Grain, or other variety with the Best Life seal, crushed

2 tablespoons roughly chopped walnuts

Combine all the ingredients in a medium bowl and serve. (For a softer consistency, let sit for 15 minutes to 1 hour.)

PREP TIME: 5 minutes   TOTAL TIME: 5 minutes

PER SERVING, ABOUT: Calories: 409  Protein: 18 g
Carbohydrate: 68 g  Dietary Fiber: 11 g  Sugars: 38 g
Total Fat: 9 g  Saturated Fat: 1 g  Cholesterol: 2 mg
Calcium: 491 mg  Sodium: 261 mg

# Buffalo with Blackberries

*Serves 4*

BUFFALO ISN'T AVAILABLE everywhere, but if you can get it, it's an extremely lean and healthy red meat choice. Even if it's not sold near you, you could always order it online. You can also substitute beef rib eye for the buffalo in this recipe.

2 cups fresh blackberries, or frozen, defrosted at room temperature

2 tablespoons minced red onion

2 tablespoons balsamic vinegar

1 tablespoon extra virgin olive oil

⅛ teaspoon salt

Black pepper to taste

1 pound buffalo ribeye, cut into 4 steaks, about 4 ounces each, at room temperature

Vegetable oil cooking spray

1. Combine the blackberries, onion, vinegar, oil, salt, and pepper in a medium bowl.
2. Heat a large heavy-bottomed skillet over medium heat.
3. Coat the meat with cooking spray and cook in the skillet for 3 minutes. Flip the meat and cook for an additional 3 minutes, or until the internal temperature reaches 130°F. The time will vary, depending on the thickness of the meat. Buffalo meat is extremely

lean; cooking it on the rare to medium-rare side will ensure that it's most tender.

4. Place the individual steaks on plates and top with the blackberry mixture. Serve.

PREP TIME: 10 minutes   TOTAL TIME: 16 minutes

PER SERVING, ABOUT: Calories: 183 Protein: 25 g
Carbohydrate: 9 g Dietary Fiber: 4 g Sugars: 5 g
Total Fat: 5 g Saturated Fat: 1 g Cholesterol: 0 mg
Calcium: 28 mg Sodium: 124 mg

# Roasted Broccoli with Balsamic Vinegar

*Serves 4*

ROASTING BROCCOLI AT a high temperature results in a delicious side dish of one of the healthiest foods in existence. Broccoli is available throughout the year, but if you get a chance buy it in season from your local farmers' market.

1 broccoli head, broken into approximately 1-inch florets
Vegetable oil cooking spray
4 cloves roasted garlic
½ teaspoon salt
2 tablespoons balsamic vinegar

1. Heat the oven to broil.
2. Coat the broccoli with cooking spray and place on a sheet pan. Cook in the oven for 4 minutes, stirring after 2 minutes. Toss the broccoli with the garlic, salt, and vinegar. Serve.

PREP TIME: 5 minutes   TOTAL TIME: 10 minutes

PER SERVING, ABOUT: Calories: 51 Protein: 3 g
Carbohydrate: 10 g Dietary Fiber: 3 g
Sugars: 3 g Total Fat: 0 g Saturated Fat: 0 g
Cholesterol: 0 mg Calcium: 61 mg Sodium: 113 mg

# Celery with Creamy Herb Dip

*Serves 1*

THIS SNACK IS easy to make ahead and take with you on the road or to the office.

6 tablespoons nonfat ricotta cheese
½ teaspoon finely chopped fresh thyme, or your favorite herb
½ teaspoon olive oil
5 stalks celery

1. Combine the ricotta, thyme, and oil in a small bowl.
2. Serve the dip with celery.

PREP TIME: 5 minutes   TOTAL TIME: 5 minutes

PER SERVING, ABOUT: Calories: 164  Protein: 13 g
Carbohydrate: 8 g  Dietary Fiber: 2 g  Sugars: 5 g
Total Fat: 9 g  Saturated Fat: 1 g  Cholesterol: 8 mg
Calcium: 348 mg  Sodium: 216 mg

# Poached Wild Salmon with Zucchini and Mustard

*Serves 4*

WILD SALMON, WHICH is available fresh from spring through September, is one of the best foods for your body; it is loaded with heart-healthy omega-3 fatty acids and essential vitamins and minerals. Try this simple poaching technique that highlights the naturally flavorful fish.

Vegetable oil cooking spray

2 onions, sliced

1 pound zucchini, sliced

2 tablespoons grainy mustard

2 tablespoons olive oil

1/4 teaspoon salt

1 tablespoon finely chopped chives

1 cup dry white wine

1 cup water

1 pound wild salmon, cut into 4 pieces, about 4 ounces each

Juice of 2 lemons

1. Heat a large heavy-bottomed skillet over medium heat. Coat with cooking spray, add the onions, and cook until translucent, about 5 minutes.
2. Add the zucchini and cook for 5 minutes, stirring constantly. Remove the onions and zucchini from the pan and place in a medium mixing bowl. Toss with mustard, oil, salt, and chives. Set aside.

3. In a large frying pan, bring the wine and water to a boil. Reduce the heat to low and simmer. Add the salmon, cover, and cook until the fish is just cooked through, 3 to 5 minutes, depending on thickness. Make a small cut and peek in the middle of the fillet; make sure that most of the deep orange color is gone. Take care not to overcook as the fish will continue cooking even after it is removed from the pan.
4. Remove the salmon immediately from the cooking liquid and put on individual plates. Squeeze the lemon juice on the fish. Serve with zucchini.

PREP TIME: 10 minutes   TOTAL TIME: 25 minutes

PER SERVING, ABOUT: Calories: 287  Protein: 25 g
Carbohydrate: 12 g  Dietary Fiber: 2 g
Sugars: 5 g  Total Fat: 15 g  Saturated Fat: 2 g
Cholesterol: 62 mg  Calcium: 55 mg  Sodium: 307 mg

# Angel Hair Pasta with Walnuts and Peas

*Serves 4*

QUELL A PASTA craving with this vegetarian dish, which provides high-quality protein thanks to Barilla PLUS. Walnuts also contribute some protein and healthy omega-3 fats as well.

1 cup walnuts

6 cloves roasted garlic, or more to taste

$\frac{1}{2}$ cup basil, ripped into small pieces

$\frac{1}{3}$ cup water

7 ounces ($\frac{1}{2}$ package) Barilla PLUS thin spaghetti, cooked
    according to package instructions

2 cups fresh peas, or frozen, defrosted at room temperature

$\frac{1}{8}$ teaspoon salt

Black pepper to taste

Red pepper flakes to taste (optional)

1. Combine the walnuts, garlic, basil, and water in a food processor for 1 minute.
2. Toss the walnut mixture with the hot cooked pasta, peas, salt, pepper, and red pepper flakes, if desired, and serve.

PREP TIME: 10 minutes    TOTAL TIME: 10 minutes

PER SERVING, ABOUT: Calories: 442 Protein: 15 g
Carbohydrate: 53 g Dietary Fiber: 11 g Sugars: 7 g
Total Fat: 21 g Saturated Fat: 2 g Cholesterol: 0 mg
Calcium: 63 mg Sodium: 296 mg

# Pan-Roasted Shrimp with Lemon, Garlic, and Spinach

*Serves 4*

LOOKING FOR A fast recipe that tastes like you've been slaving over a stove all day long? Try this dish! Pair it with a side of whole grain pasta, brown rice, or other whole grain.

4 cups spinach, well washed
4 cloves garlic, minced
Vegetable oil cooking spray
1 pound raw shrimp, shelled and deveined
Juice of 1 lemon
1 tablespoon extra virgin olive oil
⅛ teaspoon salt
Black pepper to taste

1. Place the spinach in a large bowl. Set aside.
2. Heat a large heavy-bottomed skillet over medium-low heat.
3. Coat the garlic with cooking spray and cook in the skillet until slightly browned, about 3 minutes.
4. Coat the shrimp with cooking spray.
5. Increase the heat to medium and add the shrimp, cooking on each side for 2 minutes.
6. Put the shrimp in the bowl with the spinach and toss with lemon juice, oil, salt, and pepper. Serve.

PREP TIME: 3 minutes    TOTAL TIME: 10 minutes

PER SERVING, ABOUT: Calories: 173  Protein: 24 g
Carbohydrate: 5 g  Dietary Fiber: 1 g
Sugars: 1 g  Total Fat: 7 g  Saturated Fat: 1 g
Cholesterol: 172 mg  Calcium: 98 mg  Sodium: 265 mg

**JOURNAL**

Write down your daily activities:

What did you eat?

_____

_____

_____

_____

_____

_____

Did you exercise? For how long?

_____

_____

_____

_____

Notes:

_____

_____

_____

# active™ JOURNAL

### Write down your daily activities:

What did you eat?

_____

_____

_____

_____

_____

Did you exercise? For how long?

_____

_____

_____

Notes:

_____

_____

_____

 **active** ™ JOURNAL

Write down your daily activities:

What did you eat?

_____

_____

_____

_____

_____

_____

Did you exercise? For how long?

_____

_____

_____

Notes:

_____

_____

_____

**active™ JOURNAL**

Write down your daily activities:

What did you eat?

_____

_____

_____

_____

_____

Did you exercise? For how long?

_____

_____

_____

_____

Notes:

_____

_____

_____

**active™ JOURNAL**

Write down your daily activities:

What did you eat?

_____

_____

_____

_____

_____

Did you exercise? For how long?

_____

_____

_____

Notes:

_____

_____

active™ JOURNAL

Write down your daily activities:

What did you eat?

_____

_____

_____

_____

_____

Did you exercise? For how long?

_____

_____

_____

Notes:

_____

_____

_____

## EA SPORTS active™ JOURNAL

Write down your daily activities:

What did you eat?

_____

_____

_____

_____

_____

Did you exercise? For how long?

_____

_____

_____

Notes:

_____

_____

active™ JOURNAL

Write down your daily activities:

What did you eat?

_____

_____

_____

_____

_____

Did you exercise? For how long?

_____

_____

_____

Notes:

_____

_____

_____

# active™ JOURNAL

### Write down your daily activities:

What did you eat?

_____

_____

_____

_____

_____

Did you exercise? For how long?

_____

_____

_____

Notes:

_____

_____

_____

**JOURNAL**

Write down your daily activities:

What did you eat?

_____

_____

_____

_____

_____

Did you exercise? For how long?

_____

_____

_____

Notes:

_____

_____

_____

# active™ JOURNAL

Write down your daily activities:

What did you eat?

_____

_____

_____

_____

_____

_____

Did you exercise? For how long?

_____

_____

_____

Notes:

_____

_____

### JOURNAL

Write down your daily activities:

What did you eat?

_____

_____

_____

_____

_____

Did you exercise? For how long?

_____

_____

_____

Notes:

_____

_____

_____

 **active™** JOURNAL

Write down your daily activities:

What did you eat?

_____

_____

_____

_____

_____

_____

Did you exercise? For how long?

_____

_____

_____

_____

Notes:

_____

_____

_____

**active™ JOURNAL**

Write down your daily activities:

What did you eat?

_____

_____

_____

_____

_____

Did you exercise? For how long?

_____

_____

_____

Notes:

_____

_____

_____

## active™ JOURNAL

Write down your daily activities:

What did you eat? _____

_____

_____

_____

_____

_____

Did you exercise? For how long? _____

_____

_____

_____

Notes: _____

_____

_____

## JOURNAL

Write down your daily activities:

What did you eat?

_____

_____

_____

_____

_____

Did you exercise? For how long?

_____

_____

_____

Notes:

_____

_____

active™ JOURNAL

Write down your daily activities:

What did you eat?

_____

_____

_____

_____

_____

Did you exercise? For how long?

_____

_____

_____

Notes:

_____

_____

_____